Stages
through the
Ages

David Hunt

OXFORD
UNIVERSITY PRESS

is a department of the University of Oxford.
It furthers the University's objective of excellence in research, scholarship,
and education by publishing worldwide in

Oxford   New York
Auckland   Cape Town   Dar es Salaam   Hong Kong   Karachi
Kuala Lumpur   Madrid   Melbourne   Mexico City   Nairobi
New Delhi   Shanghai   Taipei   Toronto

With offices in

Argentina   Austria   Brazil   Chile   Czech Republic   France   Greece
Guatemala   Hungary   Italy   Japan   Poland   Portugal   Singapore
South Korea   Switzerland   Thailand   Turkey   Ukraine   Vietnam

Oxford is a registered trade mark of Oxford University Press
in the UK and in certain other countries

British Library Cataloguing in Publication Data

Data available

ISBN: 978-0-19-846117-3

3 5 7 9 10 8 6 4

Printed in China

Paper used in the production of this book is a natural,
recyclable product made from wood grown in sustainable forests.
The manufacturing process conforms to the environmental
regulations of the country of origin

Acknowledgements

The publisher would like to thank the following for permission to reproduce photographs: **p4** David
Hancock/Alamy; **p5** Mediastream Film, Neal H. Moritz/Album/AKG – Images; **p6** Stone/Getty Images;
p7t Everett Collection/Rex Features, **p7**b Live Press Agency/Rex Features

Cover photograph: Alamy/Visual Arts Library (London)

Illustrations by Philip Hood/Arena: **p8/9**, **p10/11**, **p12/13**, **p14/15**, **p16/17**, **p18/19**, **p20/21**, **p22/23**;
Carol Jonas; **p3**, **p9**, **p11**, **p13**, **p15**, **p17**, **p19**, **p21**, **p23**

Contents

Introduction

Have you ever made up stories with your friends? Have you ever pretended to be the people (characters) in those stories and acted them out? Have you found costumes to wear, or used things to make the stories more realistic? Congratulations – you are an actor. You have made a make-believe world seem real.

Now imagine playing a game of make-believe in front of your whole class. Everyone is looking at you. It is your job to act out a story. We call this 'acting out' a play. The people watching and listening to a play are called the audience. This is what happens in a theatre – a place where make-believe worlds become real.

I'm sure you have seen people acting in a film, or on television. You may think television is better than a play, and it's true that film and television can do things a play can't do.

But theatre can do things that television cannot. When you go to the theatre you are seeing a live performance. The story you are watching is happening in front of you.

You usually watch television at home. You watch it on your own, with friends, or with your family. In a theatre you are part of a bigger audience. A play can be exciting, or funny, or scary. You share your excitement, laughter, or fear with the rest of the audience. This is exciting for the actors on stage as well. They react to the audience. Actors in films or on television can't do this.

Which is more exciting – watching your favourite pop group, or football team on television, or going to see them play live?

Imagine a play where the story takes place in a wood. A film or a television programme can show a real wood. So how can you show a wood in the theatre? The trick is to make the audience *feel* it's in a wood. A play can use **scenery** or **lighting effects**. But the actors must use their imagination to make a wood for the audience, and the audience must use theirs to believe they are in that wood. When it's done really well it's like watching a magic trick.

Welcome to our theatre!

This is our theatre. Let's use it to travel back to different times in history. We shall see how people used their imagination to put on plays.

A play can take you anywhere, if you use your imagination. In some ways theatre is very like a time machine. People have been writing and performing plays for thousands of years. We can still watch these old plays today. We can hear the words and watch stories that audiences heard and watched hundreds of years ago. A play can show us how we are the same and how we are different from people long ago.

Cats have always had a special place in the theatre. They lived backstage and were thought to be good luck - and they frightened the mice away!

Dogs have also had a special place in the theatre, and sometimes it was on stage as part of a play!

This is Edie Puss and Rex. When it comes to the theatre, they've seen it all. I'm sure they'll have plenty to say for themselves.

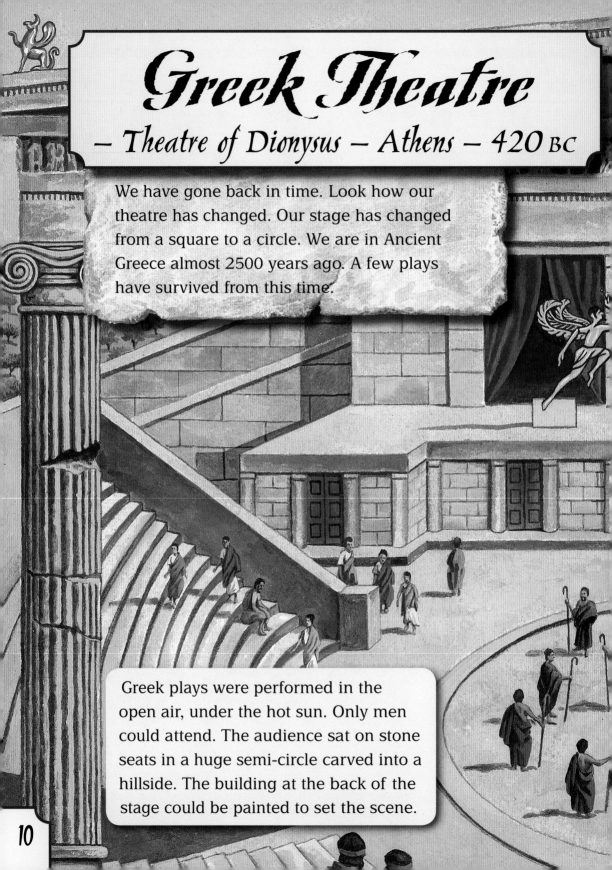

Greek Theatre

– Theatre of Dionysus – Athens – 420 BC

We have gone back in time. Look how our theatre has changed. Our stage has changed from a square to a circle. We are in Ancient Greece almost 2500 years ago. A few plays have survived from this time.

Greek plays were performed in the open air, under the hot sun. Only men could attend. The audience sat on stone seats in a huge semi-circle carved into a hillside. The building at the back of the stage could be painted to set the scene.

Each play had a large **chorus** but only three actors. The three actors played all the parts. They used masks and costumes for the different characters. Imagine all the quick changes!

The Greeks liked special effects. Characters could rise out of tunnels under the stage. There were also flying machines, or cranes. The actor playing a Greek god always flew. But the crane could also be used to 'fly in' other characters, such as winged horses. One comedy even had a flying dung beetle!

All Greek plays have a chorus to explain the story to the audience. The chorus were all young men, but because they wore masks they could play old men, or even women.

In some comic plays the chorus dressed up as creatures such as birds, wasps, frogs or dolphins. In one play they even dressed up as clouds!

Medieval Theatre

– The streets of York – England – 1416

We are not in a theatre at all. We are standing on the street in York 600 years ago watching a procession of wagons. There is a stage on each one. Each wagon stops in front of us, and a play is performed. Then the wagon moves on.

The plays told stories from the Bible. If you stood in one place from dawn until nightfall you could watch 49 plays!

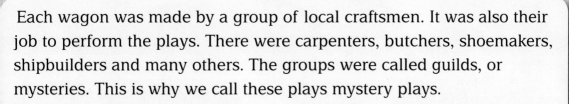

Each wagon was made by a group of local craftsmen. It was also their job to perform the plays. There were carpenters, butchers, shoemakers, shipbuilders and many others. The groups were called guilds, or mysteries. This is why we call these plays mystery plays.

Each guild wanted its play to be the best. The wagons were colourful and the costumes beautifully made. As well as trap doors, cranes for flying, and masks, they used puppets and even live animals. Blazing torches lighted some scenes. Gunpowder was used to make explosions. Even water could be pumped on to the stage to create a flood!

Each group of craftsmen chose a play where their skills would be useful. The goldsmiths performed the nativity play because they could provide expensive gifts for baby Jesus.

Can you guess which guild used to perform the play about Noah's ark?

Elizabethan Theatre
– The Globe Theatre – London – 1596

It is 1596 and Elizabeth I is Queen.
We are still in the open air but around us is a
large timber building. The stage has doors, a
balcony, and a roof called a canopy.

You could pay to sit in one of the galleries, but it was
cheaper to stand with the crowds in front of the stage.
Very rich people could sit on the stage itself!

The Elizabethan theatre was the age of the great
playwrights. The most famous was William Shakespeare.
He is as popular today as he was in his own time.

Women were allowed in the audience, but they were forbidden to act by law. This could have been a problem because Elizabethan plays had great **roles** for women, such as Juliet in *Romeo and Juliet*. The answer was to use boy actors in the women's roles.

Along with great plays, came great stage effects. There were ghosts, monsters, fairies and devils. Sword fights were staged with fake blood and gory injuries. Real guns were often fired and fireworks set off. It was the firing of a cannon which burned this theatre to the ground in 1613.

The **plague** was a serious problem. Whenever there was an outbreak the theatres had to close down.

Salomon Pavey was one of the most famous boy actors. Sadly, he died when he was just 13 years old, probably from the plague.

Jacobean Theatre
– Blackfriars Theatre – London – 1605

We are now in the Blackfriars Theatre. The stage itself hasn't changed much. The main difference is that the theatre is indoors.

Although outdoor theatres such as The Globe continued, a new type of theatre was becoming more popular. The indoor theatre was much more comfortable and weather was no longer a problem. However, it was much smaller and fewer people could watch a performance. It could cost as much as half a crown to buy a ticket for the play. Most people didn't earn that much in a month!

Indoor theatres had less light than the outdoor theatres, so they had to use candles to light the stage. This meant they could perform a play at any time. Candles also helped to create a mysterious atmosphere. The age of theatre lighting had begun.

Although Shakespeare was still writing, there were a number of other playwrights who became popular. They created plays especially for the indoor theatre, and these plays were often dark and mysterious.

There were other advantages to using candles. Because only the stage was lit, the audience watched the play and not each other!

Two of the most famous of the Jacobean playwrights were Thomas Middleton and John Webster, who wrote plays full of ghosts and spirits, blood, violence and revenge.

Restoration Theatre

– Theatre Royal, Drury Lane – London – 1671

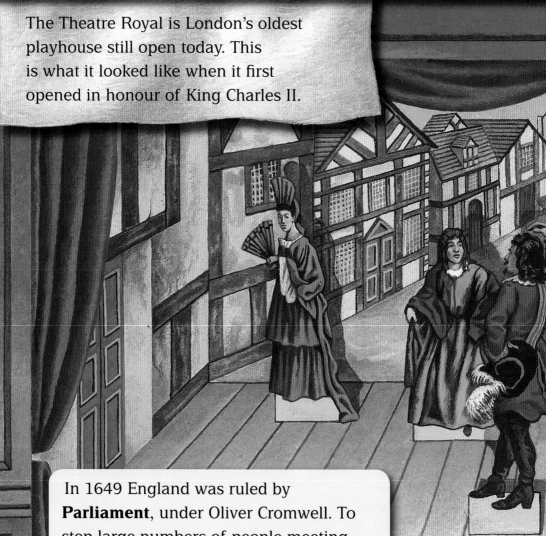

The Theatre Royal is London's oldest playhouse still open today. This is what it looked like when it first opened in honour of King Charles II.

In 1649 England was ruled by **Parliament**, under Oliver Cromwell. To stop large numbers of people meeting together, Cromwell closed all theatres. But after ten years, Prince Charles was restored to the throne, as King Charles II. These times are called the Restoration.

Charles loved the theatre. In France he had seen women acting in plays, so he passed laws allowing English women to act in public too. Nell Gwyn was the most famous actress of her time and King Charles was very fond of her. The Restoration was the age of the actress.

The players' costumes were made of the very best materials – silks, velvets, satins, and lace. Their costumes and wigs were more elaborate and expensive than anything worn in real life! Movements and gestures made by the actors were larger than life too. Each gesture had a meaning the audience would understand – rather like ballet today. If the audience didn't like what they saw, they would throw oranges at the actors!

Look at the backcloth. It's painted to make the scene look real. **Perspective** is used to make the scene seem bigger and deeper.

The Proscenium Arch frames the action on the stage, making it seem like a picture.

Victorian Theatre

– The Covent Garden Theatre – London 1867

We've moved on 200 years to the Covent Garden Theatre. Now there are theatres all over Britain. Welcome to the Victorian Age!

The Victorians were good at inventing things. Machines were used to create amazing effects. People started going to the theatre to see the special effects rather than the play. Bruce 'Sensation' Smith was a theatre inventor. His inventions showed chariot races and a ship sinking. Once he showed a train crash. It was so realistic the audience shouted to the actors to get out of the way!

Gas was used to light the stage. Gas is much brighter than candlelight but it is smelly and dangerous. Many theatres burned down in the 1800s.

Electricity was used for the first time, but not for lighting. It was used to create sparks during sword fights. The audience were said to be shocked by the experience!

Other types of theatre were popular too. You may have heard of pantomime, circus, melodrama and music hall. But have you heard of cup-and-saucer dramas? This risky sort of theatre showed *real* things happening on stage. One play showed a roly-poly pudding being made as part of the action. The audience went wild!

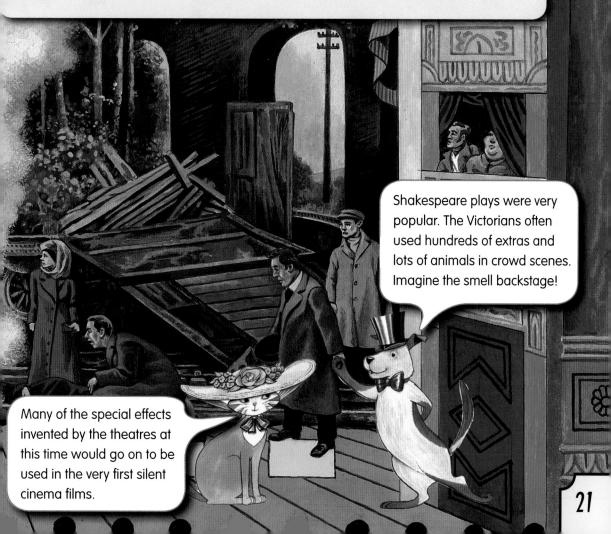

Shakespeare plays were very popular. The Victorians often used hundreds of extras and lots of animals in crowd scenes. Imagine the smell backstage!

Many of the special effects invented by the theatres at this time would go on to be used in the very first silent cinema films.

Modern Theatre and beyond

– Any theatre – Your town

Many things have changed in the 20th century and early 21st century. It is the same for theatre too. Things are changing all the time.

Throughout this time theatre was *used* for change too. Theatre was very **political**. This means that lots of different groups used theatre as a way of putting across a point of view. They wanted to change people's minds. For example, in the 1920s women wanted more rights. They put on plays as part of their protest. During the two world wars the government used theatre to keep people's spirits up. Towards the end of the 20th century a lot of playwrights wrote plays that **criticised** modern life.

Today, new plays are being written and performed all the time. Old plays from all the theatres we have read about are just as popular as ever. But what about the future?

There have been many changes in theatre technology. Recently, a lot of the lighting, special effects, make-up and costume ideas have come from film and television. Computers are used a lot in theatre.

Look at our theatre now. It's just an outline. That's because we don't know how our story ends. In fact it doesn't end. It will be up to you to decide where the theatre goes next!

Why not make a start? You can trace the outline of this theatre on to a piece of paper. Think of a story you want to tell. Imagine how you can make a play of it. Then you can design your own sets and costumes on the paper.

Start playing!

Glossary

chorus – a group of men who explained things to an audience by using speech, song and dance

criticise – to find fault in something

lighting effects – any kind of man-made lighting used to light a stage

Parliament – a meeting of the Lords and important men of England. They met to help run the country

perspective – a trick used in drawing to give a sense of distance

plague – Bubonic plague, also known as The Black Death, is a deadly disease spread by fleas

playwright – a writer of plays. 'Wright' means craftsman

political – debate about how best to run the country

role – a performer's part in a play

scenery – any object put on stage that helps to create the world of the play

Index